31 Scriptural Secrets that will Improve your Prayer Life

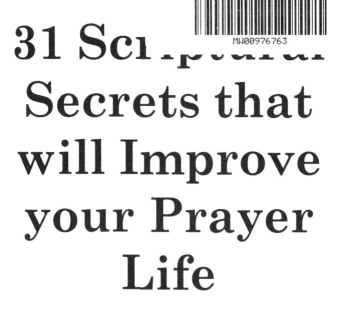

Treasures *of* Wisdom Devotional

ANDRE THOMAS

GREATNESS
PUBLISHING

www.12slm.org

Published by Greatness Publishing, Ontario, Canada

Cover design and formatting by Farouk Roberts

Library and Archives Canada

ISBN-13: 978-1541046245

All Scripture quotations are from the King James Version of the Bible, except otherwise stated.

www.greatnesspublishing.com

Acknowledgements

Thanks to my wife Nina Thomas for typing this
manuscript.

Farouk Roberts for his graphic design and the

Wisdom Epistle Team of

Cathy-Ann Forde and Trudy Waterman

for the proofreading and editing.

Last but not least, I praise the Lord Jesus Christ for
entrusting me with Wisdom for Visionaries in my
lifetime.

Introduction

Dear Reader,

You are holding this life changing devotional in your hand because of an encounter I had with the Lord in 2006.

In this encounter, the audible voice of the Lord came twice to me and said:

'The problems of this world can be solved by the people of this world if they manifest vision.'

Then the voice of the Holy Spirit spoke from within and said:

- "The problems of a generation will never be greater than the ideas and solutions within people born into that generation.
- These ideas and solutions are within people in the form of an uncommon vision.
- Except the wisdom in the visionary matches the vision, the vision will become the object of the visionary's frustration.
- I am sending you to take wisdom to Visionaries."

In June 2016 the Holy Spirit referencing Col. 2:3 "in whom are hidden all the treasures of wisdom and knowledge," instructed me to write a Wisdom Epistle to my generation that will contain an A to Z of how to fulfil Vision and call it **Treasures of Wisdom Devotional**. This is the manifestation of it.

For each day of the month, I have shared treasures of the hidden wisdom and knowledge of God for your glory, breakthrough, advancement, prosperity, healing, wholeness, greatness and the fulfilment of God's plan for your life.

1 Cor. 2:6-7:"But, we speak wisdom among those who are perfect; yet not the wisdom of this world, nor of the rulers of this world, that come to nothing. (7) But we speak the wisdom of God in a mystery, which God has hidden, predetermining it before the world for our glory;"

As you apply what you learn from the daily devotions, your life will become a wonder and the greatest version of you will appear and bring great pleasure to God as your light shines in a dark world.

For your Greatness,

Bishop Andre Thomas

Day 1

God Owns the Earth but Man Has the Lease and Dominion

Gen 1:26 And God said, Let us make man in our image, after our likeness: and let them have dominion over the fish of the sea, and over the fowl of the air, and over the cattle, and over all the earth, and over every creeping thing that creepeth upon the earth.

Understanding the mind-set of God when He created man is critical to understanding the place of prayer in God's heart and man's life.

God made the earth and therefore owns the earth. However, by the legal decree of His words, He gave man dominion over the earth. The word 'dominion' means to take charge, to rule, manage, oversee, lead and govern. In other words, God as the landlord of the earth, gave man a lease to manage the earth. This is an important concept to understand.

This is the reason why God did not intervene when Adam and Eve made the bad decision to yield to the temptation of Satan and eat from the fruit of the tree of knowledge of good and evil. God did not intervene because doing that would be like your landlord intervening in a bad decision that you made, to bring an old romantic flame into your house to live, until he/she got their finances sorted out while you are engaged to somebody else. It would be unthinkable for your landlord to get involved in that.

You now manage the house and what you do in the house is your business. To get the landlord involved in your day to day affairs, you would have to invite the landlord into your house and ask him for his advice, or tell him what contribution you would want from him.

By the same token, God Almighty would only enter the affairs of man when He is invited. This invitation given to God to intervene in the affairs of man is called 'prayer.' If you or someone else does not ask Him to come into your life, He wouldn't, as this would be a violation of the dominion He has given you.

We know that landlords conduct periodic inspections of their properties until the lease runs out; so does God. He comes to see how we are managing, administrating and governing the life on the earth He has given us. This will continue until man's lease on the earth runs out at the second coming of Jesus Christ. Until then,

God's activity on the earth is dependent on man's prayers.

Prayer

Heavenly Father, help me to understand the power of prayer and impart into me a spirit of prayer. I realize that I cannot delegate my prayer responsibilities to others. I must take responsibility to give You licence to operate in my life. In Jesus' name. Amen.

Today's Assignment

Stop and reflect.

Are you praying at the level that is required to see all of God's plan for your life come to pass? Are you hoping that He moves on your behalf even though you are not spending quality time in prayer - or are you attempting to delegate your prayer responsibility to someone else?

Day 2

Prayer is giving God earthly licence for transacting heavenly business and intervention on earth.

Psa 115:16 The heaven, even the heavens, are the LORD'S: but the earth hath he given to the children of men.

The heavens belong to God, but the earth belongs to the children of men. Heaven is magnificent beyond human words because God is in charge. Earth is a cocktail of the good, the bad, the wonderful and the evil because man is in charge. In Heaven, there are no accidents, rapes, thefts, murders, hunger, sickness, poverty or stagnation, because God Almighty is in charge. Many people, because of their spiritual illiteracy, ignorantly blame God for the bad, ugly and evil things that happen in their lives and on the earth.

Spiritually speaking, this is like blaming the landlord when your fiancé enters your house unexpectedly and catches you in bed with your old flame. That would be

4

preposterous, even though you claim he owns the house so he should have stopped it. Your landlord, even though he is a good, loving and gracious man, would not be able to stop that. You would have to give him permission to evict your old flame from the house, talk some sense into your head and inspire you to focus on making the best of your current relationship.

By the same token, the evil in life and in the earth cannot be stopped unless man prays.

This is because Satan also carries out an agenda on the earth through the art of Witchcraft, which God alludes to in the following scripture.

Num 23:23 Surely there is no enchantment against Jacob, neither is there any divination against Israel: according to this time it shall be said of Jacob and of Israel, What hath God wrought!

Witchcraft is the use of divination and enchantment to give licence to Satan and his demons to carry out their agenda to steal, kill and destroy on the earth. John 10:10 records Jesus as saying, 'the thief cometh to steal, kill and destroy but I have cometh that you may have life and have it more abundantly.'

Divination is communicating with evil spirits to obtain information about Satan's plans, prophecies and objectives in the lives of people, families and nations. It also includes communicating with demons to obtain information that demons have on people and nations.

Enchantment is using incantations and rituals to release demons on the earth, to carry out the agenda that divination has revealed. It also includes the casting of spells to destroy the destinies of people, families and nations.

Witchcraft is simply praying and making requests to the devil. Since man has dominion on earth, Satan cannot just come into the earth and do what he wants to do. Man has to allow him to come in and use him to steal, kill and destroy.

A child of God who is taking care of his/her prayer responsibilities will always defeat the forces of darkness. The light of divine intervention produced by their prayers will always expel the darkness of the demonic seeking to steal, kill and destroy them.

One of the words used to describe Satan is 'thief.' He doesn't own anything; he enters in by stealth to steal from the people of the earth. He will always be defeated through accurate prayer.

Our nations are full of covens, lodges and satanic gatherings that on a daily basis give licence to demonic intervention. It is time we switched on the light of prayer and let God arise and His enemies be scattered.

Darkness has never won a fight with God, so when the agents of Satan pray and God's people pray, there is no contest. However, if you are sleeping and snoring while satanic agents are praying— you will be defeated. Not because God is weak, but because you have not switched on the light through prayer.

Prayer

Holy Spirit, I register for training in the school of prayer. Teach me how to release the light of divine revelation and intervention in my life and affairs, so that the darkness of evil will flee from me.

Today's Assignment

The bible says to pray without ceasing and now you know why. How often do you pray?

Day 3

God only controls on earth what man gives Him licence to control through prayer, faith and obedience

Psa 115:16 The heaven, even the heavens, are the LORD'S: but the earth hath he given to the children of men.

A very popular statement that is lobbied in circles is that 'God is in control.' Many times, that couldn't be further from the truth. God does not have dominion on the earth. He has given man free will. He only controls what we give Him control over through our obedience, prayers and faith.

God was not in control when:

- Eve gave Adam the fruit from the tree of knowledge of good and evil.
- Noah's generation rebelled against Him and it caused Him to destroy them by a flood.

8

- After the flood, the children of men started to build the tower of Babel under the leadership of Nimrod.
- The children of Israel who were delivered from Egypt refused to obey His voice, which caused them to not enter Canaan Land.
- After acquiring the land of Canaan, the children of Israel rebelled against Him and followed idols, resulting in them being scattered into all nations.
- Herod beheaded John the Baptist.

God is in control of the harvest of our actions. He does not control our actions, but makes sure that every person, relationship, family, organization, town and city of a nation reap what they sow. He is the Lord of the harvest. The following scripture explains the law of reaping and sowing.

Gal 6:7-9 Do not be deceived, God is not mocked, whatsoever a man sows, that will he also reap. For he who sows to his flesh will of the flesh reap corruption. But he who soweth unto the spirit will of the spirit reap abundant life. And let us not grow weary while doing good for in due season we shall reap if we do not lose heart.

If God was in control, Jesus Christ would not have asked us to pray 'that thy will be done as it is done in heaven.'

Prayer

Heavenly Father, teach me how to give you the license to make my life a reflection of the beauty and magnificence of heaven, through my obedience, faith and prayers. In the name of Jesus.

Today's Assignment

Stop and reflect on whether you are doing enough to give God control over your life.

Day 4

Prayer is first a benefit to God before it is a benefit to us.

Jer 33:3 Call unto me, and I will answer thee, and shew thee great and mighty things, which thou knowest not.

John Wesley, a great preacher, famously said that God cannot do anything on earth except man prays. The great, mighty, marvellous, exceedingly, abundantly above all we can ask or think, things that God wants to do in our lives, families, organizations, towns, cities and nations are at the mercy of our prayer life. He is limited by our prayer life, obedience and faith.

Psa 78:41 Yea, they turned back and tempted God, and limited the Holy One of Israel.

God calls prayerlessness a sin. This is because it stops him from moving in our lives and accomplishing His great, marvellous and mighty plans.

Prayer

Heavenly Father, I ask you in the name of Jesus that you deliver me from the sin of prayerlessness and anoint me to pray like I should.

Today's Assignment

Stop and reflect on what value you give to prayer in your life.

Day 5

The Holy Spirit helps us by giving us a Prayer Agenda that will be answered

Rom 8:26-27 Likewise the Spirit also helpeth our infirmities: for we know not what we should pray for as we ought: but the Spirit itself maketh intercession for us with groanings which cannot be uttered. (27) And he that searcheth the hearts knoweth what is the mind of the Spirit, because he maketh intercession for the saints according to the will of God.

One of the great difficulties that humans face when they want to pray is that they don't know what God wants to do in their lives or how heaven wants to flow in their lives with peace, joy, love, breakthrough fulfilment and prosperity. They just don't know and pray very general prayers such as 'God bless me,' 'God heal me,' 'God promote me' and 'God provide for me,' which doesn't do much. What they are really praying is the objective of God. But praying is asking God to carry out his plans that would make the objective a reality. The revelation of God's plan for your life is the source of your prayer life. This is where the Holy Spirit comes in.

I remember a season of my life when I lived in the USA, and I was asking God for financial provision. The Holy Spirit spoke to me at that time and said that I did not have a financial provision problem. The problem was that I had not connected with the divine relationship that He had for me.

So I changed my prayers and I started praying for God to lead me to be in the right place at the right time, to meet the divine connections that He had for me. Soon after, I met a wonderful lady of Dutch origin who co-founded an amazing company that created and supplied equipment to the US military. The company had become stagnant and had hired many consultants who had not brought about change.

During a season of prayer, about one year before I met her and moved to the USA, the Lord gave her a dream that He was sending a black strategy and organization consultant to help take the company to the next level. She had been looking for me for more than a year. We met at a conference that the Holy Spirit led me to attend and we instantly connected.

After meeting her husband, I was offered a consultant job that changed my financial situation. As you can see, the Holy Spirit was correct when He said that I did not have a money problem; I just had not connected with the person who had the money. And when I started praying to connect with them, heaven manifested in my finances.

Prayer

Holy Spirit, reveal to me the things I should be praying about for advancement and breakthrough in my life in Jesus' name.

Today's Assignment

Buy a journal and form a habit of writing down the list of things that you sense the Holy Spirit wants you to pray about.

Day 6

God's word is God's part of your prayer life

1Jn 5:14-15 And this is the confidence that we have in him, that, if we ask any thing according to his will, he heareth us: (15) And if we know that he hear us, whatsoever we ask, we know that we have the petitions that we desired of him.

God's word comes to us in two forms; the Logos and the Rhema. These two words are Greek words that are translated as the word of God in the bible, but have two different meanings. The word 'Logos' is found in the book of John 1:1, "in the beginning was the Word and the Word was with God and the Word was God." The same Word was in the beginning with God, and all things were created by Him and without Him there was nothing created that was created. The word Logos literally means "the entire council of God from Genesis to Revelation". It is the totality of all of God's communication to man. In other words, the entire bible is Logos. It reveals God's general will for mankind, which is an abundant life and the fulfilment of your divine destiny. It is you living the days of heaven on earth.

Deu 11:21 states, "That your days may be multiplied, and the days of your children, in the land which the LORD sware unto your fathers to give them, as the days of heaven upon the earth."

Therefore, you can pray to eliminate anything in your life that is like the days of hell on the earth, and you can ask God to bring the days of heaven into your life.

The word "Rhema" which can be found in the book of Romans 10:17, literally means a specific word spoken to you by God concerning a specific situation. It is the voice of God to you. Example, I heard an audible voice that directed me to go to the store where a specific lady worked so I could meet her. Subsequently, I was given a vision during a service that showed me she was my wife. There is no scripture in the bible that could have revealed to me where I could locate my wife. The Logos does not tell you that; that only comes to you by the Rhema word of God.

This Rhema, which is the voice of God to you through His word or by His Spirit, will paint a picture of the future that God has for you and wants you to pray to possess.

Therefore, effective prayer draws its agenda from the Logos and the Rhema. The Rhema of God can come to you by an impression in the spirit, vision, dream, hearing the voice of God, prophecy or inward intuition, while the Logos is the entire word of God.

In praying the Rhema, a key principal to note is that it will never violate or contradict the Logos. For example, I cannot receive a Rhema that says that the answer to my financial need is to rob a bank and an angel shall protect me, because the Logos states that man shall not steal nor covet a man's goods.

Prayer

Heavenly Father, I ask in the name of Jesus that You send me a Rhema for this season of my life.

Today's Assignment

Create a journal where you highlight all the Rhema that God has given you over the course of your life.

Day 7

Inaccurate Prayers are not answered

Jas 4:3 Ye ask, and receive not, because ye ask amiss, that ye may consume it upon your lusts.

The above scripture explains a principle of prayer that many do not understand— that you can ask amiss in prayer. The word 'amiss' is an old English word that means you can miss the target—which is God's agenda for your life.

When you pray amiss, your prayers are not answered, because prayer is asking God for what He already wants to do for you. Therefore, you cannot pray for a boyfriend that does not belong to you, for the success of a business that God has not asked you to be involved in, to get a job that God does not want you in, and you cannot pray to fix a relationship that God wants dead.

This is so important to understand. God's word in the form of the Logos and the Rhema should be the true source of our prayer life. However, our lust can become the source of our prayer life. Many do not truly understand what lust is; it is not a sexual word. It simply means, to have an itch for something that does not belong to you, is not for you and is forbidden to you.

For example, an itch to take a relationship into successful marriage that God has not sanctioned, to ask God to help you successfully relocate to a country that He has not asked you to go to, to ask God to help you buy a nicer car than your next-door neighbour's, and an itch to tell somebody off. If these itches are not resisted, they can become the source of your prayers.

Every human being must deal with an itch for the forbidden. It is the nature of the flesh. It can even be a spiritual itch to walk in an anointing or ministry that God has not given to you, or to have a position in church and society that God has not ordained for you.

James and John, the disciples of Jesus, had an itch to become the two senior members of Jesus' team in eternity. Their mother suffered from the same itch, and asked Jesus if He could appoint her two sons to sit on his left hand and right hand when he gets back to heaven. Jesus basically said that He couldn't honour their request. Please see the account of this below.

Mrk 10:35-40 And James and John, the sons of Zebedee, come unto him, saying, Master, we would that thou shouldest do for us whatsoever we shall desire. (36) And he said unto them, What would ye that I should do for you? (37) They said unto him,

Grant unto us that we may sit, one on thy right hand,
and the other on thy left hand, in thy glory. (38) But
Jesus said unto them, Ye know not what ye ask: can ye
drink of the cup that I drink of? and be baptized with
the baptism that I am baptized with? (39) And they
said unto him, We can. And Jesus said unto them, Ye
shall indeed drink of the cup that I drink of; and with
the baptism that I am baptized withal shall ye be
baptized: (40) But to sit on my right hand and on my
left hand is not mine to give; but it shall be given to
them for whom it is prepared.

John was one of the greatest of Jesus' disciples. He wrote the book of Revelation, yet he had a lust for a position that did not belong to him. Having an itch in you that God has forbidden does not make you evil. It just means that you are human, and you have a flesh that must be crucified.

Starting from today, do not allow any itches that you may have to become the source of your prayer life. Instead, let it be the Logos and the Rhema word of God.

Prayer

Heavenly Father, I ask that by the Holy Spirit, You give me the grace to crucify every itch in me that is forbidden in the name of Jesus. I declare that I will not be controlled and led by an itch for what belongs to someone else, what does not belong to me and what is forbidden to me in Jesus' Name. Amen.

Today's Assignment

Stop and reflect.

Mentally list all the itches you need to crucify that are within you. Please be mindful that the crucifixion of an itch within you is a marathon and not a sprint.

Day 8

God's word to you is the source of your prayers; however, your fervency is the power behind your prayers

Jas 5:16-18 Confess your faults one to another, and pray one for another, that ye may be healed. The effectual fervent prayer of a righteous man availeth much. (17) Elias was a man subject to like passions as we are, and he prayed earnestly that it might not rain: and it rained not on the earth by the space of three years and six months. (18) And he prayed again, and the heaven gave rain, and the earth brought forth her fruit.

For your prayers to be effective they need to be based on God's Logos and Rhema word. However, for them to have power behind them they require your fervency. The word 'fervent' means red hot. An iron does not deliver its potential until it reaches the right temperature to iron out the material, even though the iron has the required weight to do it. Without the required heat, it will not remove the wrinkles and creases in the cloth. In the same way, prayer must be hot and not cold. It must be passionate and not bland. It must be enthusiastic and not lukewarm to dismantle the forces of darkness, and release the angels of God. The bible says that Jesus prayed with strong cries. How can we get the answers to our prayers when we are lukewarm? So, stir the fire within you, lift your voice like a trumpet and pray for heaven's will to be done in your life with every fibre of your being.

Prayer must be intense as it is the birthing of the divine will of God in the earthly realm. Just like child birth is fiery red hot, so too is effective prayer.

Prayer

Heavenly Father, give me the grace to be fervent, passionate, enthusiastic and red hot; for the fervent, effective prayer of a righteous person availeth much.

Assignment

Stop and reflect on whether you are cold, lukewarm or hot in your prayers.

Day 9

Iniquity is the enemy of your Prayers

Isa 59:1-2 Behold, the LORD'S hand is not shortened, that it cannot save; neither his ear heavy, that it cannot hear: (2) But your iniquities have separated between you and your God, and your sins have hid his face from you, that he will not hear.

Sin comes in three forms— transgressions, iniquities and abominations. A Transgression is a violation of a boundary or divine law in a particular instance. An Iniquity is a habitual, unconscious, continual violation of a divine boundary and law. It is not sin by accident but a sin that has become a lifestyle. An Abomination is a sin that cannot be done without a demon directly helping you do it; it is so disgusting to God and His plan for your life.

Iniquity, which is a lifestyle of sin, will block your prayers from being answered. It will cause you to open the door to satanic activity in your life. This will be legal entry because sin is of the devil. As a consequence of the habitual sin, the devil has been invited into your life and he will stop your prayers from being answered.

This is like offering a room in your house to someone who is supposed to be your friend, but when you order your monthly supplies from Amazon.com, he answers the door upon the arrival of the UPS delivery man and tells him that he has the wrong address. When iniquity is in your life, the answer to your prayers will be resisted. Iniquity also causes God's presence and favour to lessen or withdraw totally from your life. It also strips your prayers of authority and power to change events on the earth, in your favour.

Prayer

Holy Spirit, show me if there are any transgressions, iniquities or abominations in my life. Heavenly Father, I ask in the name of Jesus that You cleanse my life from these sins. Release your grace on me so that I can break these habits and walk into Your plans and purposes.

Today's Assignment

Study your life and see if there is any pattern of iniquity in your life that originates from your tribulations or has been transferred to your children.

The reason for this is that transgressions are not transferrable but iniquity is, as detailed in the following scripture.

Num 14:18 The LORD is longsuffering, and of great mercy, forgiving iniquity and transgression, and by no means clearing the guilty, visiting the iniquity of the fathers upon the children unto the third and fourth generation.

Day 10

The art of discovering what to pray about is called 'Watching.'

Eph 6:18 Praying always with all prayer and supplication in the Spirit, and watching thereunto with all perseverance and supplication for all saints;

The word 'watch' comes from the word watchman, which in modern terms refers to a security guard. In growing up, we always had a watchman at the house. Our family home was on a property the size of a small football pitch, with a seven-foot wall and hedge around it and a large twelve-foot iron gate.

My father would hire a watchman, whose job was to open the gate when the members of the household were leaving or returning home, or when we were having visitors. He was also required to sound the alarm, and ward off and resist any thieves that would try to enter the premises. It was required that he would not sleep at night but would continuously patrol the property to ensure that we were safe within the walls. I can remember many watchmen who were fired for sleeping on the job. My dad would return home about three in the morning, open and close the twelve-foot gate, park the car in the garage and look for the watchman, only to find him sleeping on the job. He would leave him sleeping, and take the watchman's flashlight, keys and shoes with him upstairs. The next morning there would be drama in the Thomas family, as the security guard would start frantically looking for his flashlight, keys and shoes. My dad would then produce them, which resulted in the watchman begging to keep his job, to which my father's response would be a loud "YOU ARE FIRED!" The next watchman would be hired, and my siblings and I would bet on how long it would take for him to be fired for sleeping.

While this is a true and humorous story, it reveals a great principal of prayer. You are the watchman of your life. At the gate of your life, God wants to come in with breakthroughs, destiny, divine relationships, uncommon success and heaven on earth. However, you must open the gate and not be asleep when He is knocking on your door. He wants to come in.

By the same token, Satan and his demons are thieves who want to climb over the wall and creep in, to steal, kill and destroy from your life, when you are not watching. Many have failed to access what God has for them, because they are asleep to what God wants to do in their life. Many have experienced great devastation in their life, because they were asleep to what Satan wanted to steal from their life. Your watching to discern what God wants to do in your life, and what Satan wants to destroy in your life, should be your guide on how to pray. It's time to arise from your spiritual slumber. Watch and then pray. Prayer opens the gate for the divine to come into your life, and prayer closes the gate from demonic access into your life.

Prayer

Heavenly Father in the name of Jesus, forgive me for the times of spiritual slumber, when I did not open the gate of prayer for You to do the magnificent in my life. I ask that You give me the grace to watch more effectively, so that I can open the gate of prayer to Your plans, and shut the gate of prayer for the agenda of Satan for my life and my family. In Jesus' name. Amen.

Today's Assignment

Stop, reflect and grade yourself on a scale from 1 to 10 on how effectively you watch over the gate of your destiny.

Day 11

Watching and praying is the antidote to being blindsided and defeated by temptations, tests and trials.

Matt 26:40-41 And he cometh unto the disciples, and findeth them asleep, and saith unto Peter, What, could ye not watch with me one hour? (41) Watch and pray, that ye enter not into temptation: the spirit indeed is willing, but the flesh is weak.

There are battles that cannot be avoided and we must depend upon God's wisdom and grace, and Jesus' victory on the cross to walk in victory. However, there are many battles that men and women face that could have been avoided. In this scripture, Jesus was warning his disciples that they needed to watch and be alert in the spirit. They also needed to recognise that he was going to be executed on the cross, and that their lives would be under threat by the same spirit of murder.

31

He also shared with them that he knew that they did not want to be defeated by sin, fear and the forces of darkness - but if they did not detect in the spirit what was about to happen and pray to receive the grace to overcome, their weak flesh would cause them to be defeated.

This is the story of many believers who are defeated by sin and the forces of darkness. They fail to detect the presence of evil around their lives during seasons of warfare.

One of the great truths of Spiritual Warfare is to understand that evil does not attack a person all the time; it comes in seasons. I therefore encourage you to stay alert and be sensitive in the spirit to recognise when you are under attack, from the revelation that God gives you through inward perception, the still small voice, dreams and visions, and revelation from the word.

Many sleep while they are under attack and therefore are defeated. When you sense darkness and heaviness in the spirit realm, that is the time to discern the oppression and overcome it by prayer.

Many people have not been trained on how to respond to a sudden perception of darkness, evil, resistance, and heaviness in their atmosphere.

I declare that from today in the name of Jesus, that you are sensitive to the spiritual environment around you, for evil cannot enter your life in the physical realm unless evil enters your life in the spirit realm.

What happens in the physical realm is simply a print out of what has taken place in the spiritual realm. So if you stop it spiritually, it would not manifest physically.

Prayer

Heavenly Father, I ask that You anoint me to perceive all spiritual activity both divine and demonic in my life, so that I may activate the divine to manifest in the physical, and stop the demonic from manifesting in the physical.

Today's Assignment

Stop and reflect about a time that you perceived evil in the spiritual environment around you but did nothing about it. What was the result?

Day 12

Watching and praying is the divine method for escaping the evil of these perilous times, also known as the end of the last days

Luke 21:25-28 And there shall be signs in the sun, and in the moon, and in the stars; and upon the earth distress of nations, with perplexity; the sea and the waves roaring; (26) Men's hearts failing them for fear, and for looking after those things which are coming on the earth: for the powers of heaven shall be shaken. (27) And then shall they see the Son of man coming in a cloud with power and great glory. (28) And when these things begin to come to pass, then look up, and lift up your heads; for your redemption draweth nigh.

Luke 21:34-36 And take heed to yourselves, lest at any time your hearts be overcharged with surfeiting, and drunkenness, and cares of this life, and so that day come upon you unawares. (35) For as a snare shall it come on all them that dwell on the face of the whole

earth. (36) Watch ye therefore, and pray always, that
ye may be accounted worthy to escape all these things
that shall come to pass, and to stand before the Son of
man.

The end of the last days shall be a time when great
wickedness is manifested upon the earth. This
wickedness in the form of terrorism, computer hacking,
theft, drug addiction, infidelity on steroids,
pornography on steroids, economic calamity, natural
disasters, broken families, geo-political instability and
evil people will be getting worse and worse.

A look at the news reveals that this environment is
presently our daily experience. To escape becoming a
casualty of these powers would require an astuteness
and vigilance in watching over the spiritual
environment of your life.

God's power is greater than the evil of the last days, and
God's wisdom is greater than the evil of the end of the
last days. God's angels who protect us are greater than
the evil of the end of the last days. The divine weapons
of the saints such as the name of Jesus, the blood of
Jesus, the word of God and the Anointing are infinitely
greater than the end of the last days.

However, if the vigilance and the alertness of the saints
do not match the evil of the end of the last days, in the

geographical location where they live, despite the power of the divine weapons available to them they will become casualties of spiritual war.

They will not be defeated because they lack weapons; they will be defeated because when the enemy attacks them, they would be in bed snoring and unable to put up a proper fight. Let this not be applicable to you. I am persuaded that the revelation of the spirit would turn you into a man or woman that properly secures your lives and destiny.

Prayer

Heavenly Father, give me an anointing in the name of Jesus that is greater than the evil in my environment, and give me a Holy Spirit radar that can detect enemy movements against me before they land. In the name of Jesus. Amen.

Today's Assignment

Can you list three people from the scriptures, who prevented evil from destroying their lives because they were spiritually alert?

Day 13

There are different kinds of prayer solutions for differing kinds of situations

Eph 6:18 Praying always with all prayer and supplication in the Spirit, and watching thereunto with all perseverance and supplication for all saints;

Eph 6:18 ISV Pray in the Spirit at all times with every kind of prayer and request. Likewise, be alert with your most diligent efforts and pray for all the saints

There are twelve different types of prayer that fit different scenarios. Each prayer gives licence for a particular type of divine intervention. A carpenter has a variety of different tools, e.g. a saw, chisel, hammer, sandpaper, nails, tape measure, etc., and the tools work in harmony with each other, according to the wisdom of the carpenter, to create his end product.

Even so, the saints have twelve different forms of prayer available to them. They must use wisdom and understanding to know which one to use in a given scenario, to cause the will of God to be done as it is in heaven.

Many saints are ignorant of this and they think that they can pray anyhow. But each prayer is governed by different rules, just as the rules of basketball govern basketball and the rules of soccer govern soccer.

Accordingly, the rules that govern praying in the spirit do not govern the rules of decree and declaration, or the rules of enquiry.

Many people have their favourite way of praying and try to use it for every scenario of their life. This will always cause frustration because of partial results. This would be similar to a carpenter using his hammer as the only tool to try to create a set of kitchen cabinets. At the end of the day he will be a frustrated carpenter, and the kitchen cabinets will not be a reality.

By the same token, there are saints who are addicted to one form of prayer, like the prayer of supplication, and will try to use it to receive divine revelation and intervention in every sphere of life, without success.

As you read the following chapters, you will gain an understanding into the twelve types of prayer, the rules that govern them and how to achieve success when praying them.

Please note that prayer is only answered because of God's mercy and grace. Both mercy and grace can be characterized as kindness to the undeserved. However, mercy is God not giving you the punishment that you deserve, while grace is God giving you something that you don't deserve.

Those who are not merciful to the people who have trespassed against them, and are not gracious to others, will block their prayers from being answered by God. Matthew 5:7 states, "Blessed are the merciful for they shall obtain mercy."

Prayer

Holy Spirit, teach me about the different types of prayer so I can use them to unlock divine grace and mercy on my life, church, family and situations.

Today's Assignment

Stop and reflect on a scale of 1 to 10, with 1 being the lowest and 10 being the highest, on your knowledge of the principles that govern the twelve types of prayer.

Day 14

The Prayer of Faith releases the power of God to remove the mountains in your way

Mrk 11:23-26 For verily I say unto you, That whosoever shall say unto this mountain, Be thou removed, and be thou cast into the sea; and shall not doubt in his heart, but shall believe that those things which he saith shall come to pass; he shall have whatsoever he saith. (24) Therefore I say unto you, What things soever ye desire, when ye pray, believe that ye receive them, and ye shall have them. (25) And when ye stand praying, forgive, if ye have ought against any: that your Father also which is in heaven may forgive you your trespasses. (26) But if ye do not forgive, neither will your Father which is in heaven forgive your trespasses.

The Prayer of Faith is used for the things that Jesus died on the cross for you to receive instantly. These are:

- Forgiveness of sins - because He died for our sins (Isa 53).
- Healing of our bodies - because with His stripes we are healed (Isa 53).
- Deliverance from transgressions, iniquity and abominations - because He was wounded for our transgressions and bruised for our iniquities (Isa 53).
- Peace - for the chastisements for our peace was upon Him (Isa 53).
- Our financial provision - as our God shall supply all our needs according to His riches in glory (Phil 4:19).

The Prayer of Faith is supposed to deal with every mountain of obstacles, challenges, demonic interference, calamities, and evil systems that are working against you. You can command them to move from obstructing you, so that you can receive what Jesus died for you to receive.

In the Prayer of Faith, you do not speak to God; you speak to the mountain and command it to move in the name of Jesus. However, as the name suggests, it is a prayer for the release of explosive faith in God's word. Therefore, in praying the Prayer of Faith, you must take time to meditate on the scriptures that deal with your situation and receive a fresh impartation of God's faith into your spirit.

This is because faith is not stored - it has to be fresh for it to work. Even though I know virtually all the written scriptures in the bible and can quote most of them, I am not going to pray the Prayer of Faith for myself at a service - I will go back in the scriptures, meditate on them and receive a fresh impartation of faith for my healing in the spirit. Then and only then, will I pray.

Many pray the Prayer of Faith for healing, provision, peace, and deliverance from iniquities and abominations without fresh faith. That is why they see no results. In preparing to pray the Prayer of Faith, you must study and meditate on the scriptures that apply to the situation you desire to pray about, so that you can extract faith from the scriptures to use when you pray. Faith is stored in God's word. It is a spiritual substance and force that is transmitted into the human spirit when the word of God comes alive in you. (Rom 10:17 "So then faith cometh by hearing and hearing by the word of God.")

If I did not have enough money in my bank account to pay my bills, even though I know and can quote the scriptures that speak of divine provision, I would have to meditate and study those same scriptures before I can pray the Prayer of Faith.

Psa 112:1-4 Praise ye the LORD. Blessed is the man that feareth the LORD, that delighteth greatly in his commandments. (2) His seed shall be mighty upon earth: the generation of the upright shall be blessed. (3) Wealth and riches shall be in his house: and his righteousness endureth for ever. (4) Unto the upright there ariseth light in the darkness: he is gracious, and full of compassion, and righteous.

I would spend between a few hours to a few days meditating on the above scripture, until faith dropped in my spirit and all doubt is erased. Only then will I rise up to pray and declare that the mountains of a low income job, the spirit of poverty and recession in the land shall move out of my way and path so that I may receive my divine provision. For my God shall supply wealth and riches to my house, and every mountain that is stopping wealth and riches from coming to my house, will be dissolved in the name of Jesus.

Another law that governs results when praying the Prayer of Faith is forgiveness. Because faith works by love, faith cannot be released in an unforgiving heart.

In order to receive when using the Prayer of Faith,

you need to:

- pray about something that Jesus died for you to receive instantly.
- let go of stale faith and obtain fresh faith from the relevant scriptures.
- have a forgiving heart.

Prayer

Holy Spirit, I ask that You further teach me the concepts and principles of the Prayer of Faith, in Jesus' name.

Today's Assignment

Stop and reflect on an example of when you used the Prayer of Faith and did not get a result. What do you think was the reason?

Day 15

Praying in the Spirit activates the exceeding abundantly above all you can ask or think agenda of God into manifestation.

1 Cor 14:2 For he that speaketh in an unknown tongue speaketh not unto men, but unto God: for no man understandeth him; howbeit in the spirit he speaketh mysteries.

Act 2:1-12 And when the day of Pentecost was fully come, they were all with one accord in one place. (2) And suddenly there came a sound from heaven as of a rushing mighty wind, and it filled all the house where they were sitting. (3) And there appeared unto them cloven tongues like as of fire, and it sat upon each of them. (4) And they were all filled with the Holy Ghost, and began to speak with other tongues, as the Spirit gave them utterance. (5) And there were dwelling at Jerusalem Jews, devout men, out of every nation under heaven. (6) Now when this was noised abroad, the multitude came together, and were confounded, because that every man heard them speak in his own language. (7) And they were all

45

amazed and marvelled, saying one to another, Behold, are not all these which speak Galilaeans? (8) And how hear we every man in our own tongue, wherein we were born? (9) Parthians, and Medes, and Elamites, and the dwellers in Mesopotamia, and in Judaea, and Cappadocia, in Pontus, and Asia, (10) Phrygia, and Pamphylia, in Egypt, and in the parts of Libya about Cyrene, and strangers of Rome, Jews and proselytes, (11) Cretes and Arabians, we do hear them speak in our tongues the wonderful works of God. (12) And they were all amazed, and were in doubt, saying one to another, What meaneth this?

Eph 3:20 Now unto him that is able to do exceeding abundantly above all that we ask or think, according to the power that worketh in us.

There is no way your natural mind and perception can pray the details of His exceeding abundantly above all you can ask or think plan that he has for your life, family, church, city or nation.

The only way you can pray that is to let the Holy Spirit pray it for you by praying in tongues. Oh what a wonderful invention of God; praying in the spirit.

When you pray in the spirit, you are praying the perfect magnificent plan of God. This plan can then be interpreted to you by the spirit, which then illuminates your understanding and activates the genius in you.

Paul was a man of unusual revelations, and he lived an exceeding abundantly above all you can ask or think lifestyle. In 1 Corinthians 14:16, he thanked God that he prayed more in tongues than anyone in the Corinthian church; however, when he was preaching from the pulpit he would rather preach the revelations that the tongues gave him access to.

So reader, I encourage you to get filled with the Holy Spirit, and pray at least one hour in tongues every day to access the supernatural for your life.

Prayer

Oh Holy Spirit, teach me the concepts and principles of praying in the spirit, in Jesus' name. Amen.

Today's Assignment

Stop and reflect on how much time you spend praying in the Holy Spirit, to access the supernatural in your life.

Day 16

Praying in the Spirit builds up your spirit man's capacity and strength

1 Cor 14:4 He that speaketh in an unknown tongue edifieth himself; but he that prophesieth edifieth the church.

Jude 1:20 But ye, beloved, building up yourselves on your most holy faith, praying in the Holy Ghost,

Praying in the spirit also edifies your spirit. The word 'edify' means to build up or to recharge. It's what persons do to their muscles when they go to the gym, and lift weights that tighten the muscles, which helps them to grow. It also conveys the meaning of charging up a battery until it grows. Therefore, praying in the spirit builds up the spirit man to grow, and charges it with the fire and power of God.

I encourage you today to develop a lifestyle of praying in the spirit.

Prayer

Heavenly Father, I ask that You give me the grace to develop a lifestyle of praying in the spirit. In Jesus' name. Amen.

Today's Assignment

What are you going to do differently on a daily basis to ensure that you have quality time to pray in the spirit?

Day 17

Praying in the Spirit is different from the gift of diverse kinds of tongues.

Mrk 16:15-18 And he said unto them, Go ye into all the world, and preach the gospel to every creature. (16) He that believeth and is baptized shall be saved; but he that believeth not shall be damned. (17) And these signs shall follow them that believe; In my name shall they cast out devils; they shall speak with new tongues; (18) They shall take up serpents; and if they drink any deadly thing, it shall not hurt them; they shall lay hands on the sick, and they shall recover.

1 Cor 12:1-11 Now concerning spiritual gifts, brethren, I would not have you ignorant. (2) Ye know that ye were Gentiles, carried away unto these dumb idols, even as ye were led. (3) Wherefore I give you to understand, that no man speaking by the Spirit of God calleth Jesus accursed: and that no man can say that Jesus is the Lord, but by the Holy Ghost. (4) Now

there are diversities of gifts, but the same
Spirit. (5) And there are differences of
administrations, but the same Lord. (6) And there are
diversities of operations, but it is the same God which
worketh all in all. (7) But the manifestation of the
Spirit is given to every man to profit withal. (8) For to
one is given by the Spirit the word of wisdom; to
another the word of knowledge by the same
Spirit; (9) To another faith by the same Spirit; to
another the gifts of healing by the same Spirit; (10) To
another the working of miracles; to another prophecy;
to another discerning of spirits; to another divers kinds
of tongues; to another the interpretation of
tongues: (11) But all these worketh that one and the
selfsame Spirit, dividing to every man severally as he
will.

There is confusion in the body of Christ as to the rules
that govern praying in the spirit, and the diverse kinds
of tongues that should be interpreted.

The gift of 'diverse kinds of tongues' is an operation of
the Holy Spirit, where he gives a person a prophecy
from God in the prayer language of tongues, that is
meant for someone or a group of people.

Since the message is in tongues, it requires someone that has the spiritual gift of interpretation for that tongue, to be present to interpret it.

This gift of interpretation may fall upon the person who received the anointing to speak the prophecy in supernatural tongues, or it may fall on someone else in the environment who heard the message.

This is very different from the supernatural prayer language that God gives a person to pray. It is given to an individual to communicate with God in prayer and the Heavenly Father certainly understands it, so it does not require interpretation.

However, a mature individual in the spirit can ask the Heavenly Father for the interpretation of the tongues that they are praying, so they can get a sense of what they are praying about.

Many do not understand the difference between these two types of prayers. They think that they need to receive a special gift from God, to have the supernatural prayer language of the spirit. This is far from the truth - as it is available to every believer through the baptism of the Holy Spirit, with the evidence of speaking in tongues.

Prayer

Heavenly Father, empower me with the stamina to pray in tongues for a length of time, so I can prepare a highway for you to access the uncommon, unusual, spectacular and the magnificent in my life, in the name of Jesus. Amen.

Today's Assignment

Stop and reflect on the obstacles you face in developing a powerful prayer life.

.

Day 18

The Prayer of Repentance is confessing your sin to the Father, and realigning with the will of God for your life, after you have strayed from the divine path

1 John 1:6-10 If we say that we have fellowship with him, and walk in darkness, we lie, and do not the truth: (7) But if we walk in the light, as he is in the light, we have fellowship one with another, and the blood of Jesus Christ his Son cleanseth us from all sin. (8) If we say that we have no sin, we deceive ourselves, and the truth is not in us. (9) If we confess our sins, he is faithful and just to forgive us our sins, and to cleanse us from all unrighteousness. (10) If we say that we have not sinned, we make him a liar, and his word is not in us.

During your life as a citizen of the Kingdom of Heaven, you will make mistakes and break spiritual laws and principles. In other words, you will sin. The word 'sin' means to miss the mark and break a law, or to cross a boundary. When this occurs, you must follow the scriptural formula of humbly going to God in the name of Jesus and confess your sin. Do not hide or excuse your sin or blame someone else. To 'confess' means to state what your sin was and to say what you did that was wrong. You then ask the Heavenly Father for forgiveness and the grace not to do it again; this you do in faith. As you receive God's forgiveness and His grace, you get up from the place of prayer and purpose in your heart to do better.

Below is an example of a Prayer of Repentance (which means to go in the opposite direction).

"Heavenly Father, my heart is broken for I have sinned against You by embracing these thoughts, speaking these words, and carrying out these actions that are contrary to the laws of Your nature and the Kingdom of Heaven. I ask that You forgive me for my sin because of the blood of Jesus that was shed for me. That blood caused my sins to be remitted and my slate to be wiped clean. It also restored me to right standing with You. I humbly ask that You give me the grace to not fall into the pit of the same sin again, in the name of Jesus. I now receive forgiveness for my sin, and know that You have put it in the sea of forgetfulness, because Your word said that You have blotted it out of the book of the record of my life. Isa 43:25 'I, *even* I, *am* he that blotteth out thy transgressions for mine own sake, and will not remember thy sins.'

I also receive the grace to overcome this sin when it comes knocking on my door again, in the name of Jesus. Amen."

Prayer

Holy Spirit, teach me the concepts and principles of the Prayer of Repentance in Jesus' name. Amen.

Today's Assignment

Stop and reflect on whether you pray the Prayer of Repentance effectively under the burden of the guilt of past sins, iniquities and abominations.

Day 19

The Salvation Prayer transforms you from a sinner to become a child of God

Rom 10:8-9 But what saith it? The word is nigh thee, even in thy mouth, and in thy heart: that is, the word of faith, which we preach; (9) That if thou shalt confess with thy mouth the Lord Jesus, and shalt believe in thine heart that God hath raised him from the dead, thou shalt be saved.

John 1:11-13 He came unto his own, and his own received him not. (12) But as many as received him, to them gave he power to become the sons of God, even to them that believe on his name: (13) Which were born, not of blood, nor of the will of the flesh, nor of the will of man, but of God.

The Prayer of Salvation is the greatest prayer that a person can pray. It is a prayer that transforms you from being a sinner and a child of the devil, to being a child of God in the Kingdom of Heaven

Not everyone is a child of God. Let me explain. An omelette does not become my child just because I created it. A shirt does not become my child just because I sowed it. A latte does not become my child just because I made it. My child is something that I created that shares my DNA and characteristics. So, there are billions of people that do not have the divine nature, which is the DNA of God.

They are the children of the devil because they have the nature of the devil inside of them, even though they are a creation of God. Therefore, the statement that we are all God's children is a manifestation of acute spiritual illiteracy.

We must understand that the greatest spiritual illiterate is a highly educated spiritual illiterate, who has a great natural education but never registered for spiritual kindergarten, and is completely ignorant of the spiritual laws, concepts and principles that govern the kingdom - that govern the spirit realm that produces the natural.

John 3:16 For God so loved the world, that he gave his only begotten Son, that whosoever believeth in him should not perish, but have everlasting life.

The word everlasting life comes from the Greek word 'Zoe' which means the life and nature of God. It is literally God's genes that enter into a person's spirit, when he receives Jesus as his Lord and Saviour.

Some people mistakenly think that everlasting life means to live forever. That is not true as everybody will live forever. Spirits will never cease to exist, they will just live in different places. Some are in heaven in the heavenly Jerusalem, while others are in the lake of fire and brimstone with their father the devil.

The prayer that causes you to vomit the genes of the devil, and receive an impartation of the genes of God in you, is the Salvation Prayer. It is found in Rom 9:10 and can simply be prayed this way -

"Heavenly Father I come before You and I make Jesus the Saviour and Lord of my life. I repent of my sins and I receive the righteousness that Jesus died on the cross to give me. Cleanse me of the sins from my life in the name of Jesus, for I am a sinner, and put Your life in me. For I believe that you raised Jesus from the dead for my sake, and I purpose from this day to serve You and live for You in the name of Jesus. Amen.

This is the greatest prayer that a person can pray. What is the use of having God answer some of your others prayers and you end up spending the rest of eternity in the lake of fire and brimstone, in the jailhouse for all spiritual criminals with Satan and his demons? Can you imagine what it would be like to be in a place where you are surrounded by demonic spiritual criminals, and human spiritual criminals forever? Do not let anybody, any sin, any lust or any desire take you to that place where the worst of the angels and the worst of humanity dwell. It is literally the dustbin of eternity. Don't go there. Say the Salvation Prayer and do not backslide for a temporal high. It is not worth it.

Prayer

Holy Spirit, empower me to maintain my salvation and help me lead other people to salvation in Jesus' name. Also, deliver me from the evil spirit that makes people highly educated spiritual idiots. I want to be spiritually and naturally wise. In Jesus' name. Amen.

Today's Assignment

Stop and reflect on whether you have made Jesus the Lord of your life or whether you are playing Russian Roulette with your salvation.

Day 20

The Prayer of Binding and Loosing stops the operation of demons and releases the manifestation of Angels

Matt 18:18 Verily I say unto you, Whatsoever ye shall bind on earth shall be bound in heaven: and whatsoever ye shall loose on earth shall be loosed in heaven.

The Prayer of Binding and Loosing is Warfare prayer. We live in a world where there is Spiritual Warfare between fallen angels, demons, the angels of God and the saints. This raging warfare is more intense than any war ever fought on the earth. It has devastated more people than all the world wars combined. It defines -

- Whether people rise or fall.
- Whether marriages succeed or fail.
- Whether families experience hell or joy on earth.
- Whether nations attract in the prison of poverty, lack and economic slavery or whether they experience economic dignity and prosperity.

- Whether businesses expand, thrive or just go through the motions on the treadmill of activity.

You were born into a spiritual war; you can't run or hide from it.

But God did not leave you without a weapon. He has given you the authority to bind, stop and destroy the operations of evil spirits, demons and fallen angels that are coming against you and your interests. He has given you the power to release the angels of God to defend you and bring heaven's reality and breakthroughs into your life. Oh, how the devil fears this prayer.

Even while you are reading this lesson, demons are trembling as the days of their dominance over your life are coming to an end.

In your spiritual, mental, emotional, romantic, sexual, financial, health, career, social, and destiny life, there are classes of demonic specialists that attack.

However, the weapon of binding and loosing will bind from the greatest demon to the smallest demon. Metaphorically speaking, it carries a spiritual intercontinental ballistic missile of mass destruction.

It doesn't matter what kind of demon or devil it is. It doesn't matter what kind of attack is coming against you, it can be destroyed and annihilated in the name of Jesus. This is because the Prayer of Binding and

Loosing is a prayer of mass destruction. It is a Holy Ghost nuclear bomb. It can be released by you for your life. It also has intercontinental capability. That is, you can stand in Bridgetown and bind the devil in Bangkok, and it would bind.

Where possible, with the help of the Holy Spirit, the prayer requires that you identify the specific demons that are in operation. If that is not possible, use the general prayer. It also requires that you loose the spirit of God and the angels of God to go to battle on your behalf.

An example of the Prayer of Binding and Loosing for a person experiencing emotional and mental anguish is as follows -

"In the name of Jesus, the word of God declares that God has not given me the spirit of fear but of power, love and a sound mind. I will not yield to a spirit of torment, anxiety, frustration and worry in the name of Jesus. Right now, I arise in the power of the Holy Spirit and every spirit of depression, frustration, anxiety, fear, torment, suicide, self - sabotage, regret and guilt, I bind your operations against me in the name of Jesus. I command you in the name of Jesus, by the power of Jesus, to cease operations in your manoeuvres against me. I hereby release the power of the Holy Spirit against you, to destroy all your works in the name of Jesus. I loose the angels of God against you in the name of Jesus. I declare, let God arise in my emotional life and let all His enemies scatter, in the name of Jesus."

This prayer can also be prayed for a loved one who is being imprisoned by demons and going in the wrong direction. The greater the spiritual and destiny connection to the person, the more authority the prayer would have. I would have more authority praying for my child than praying for the gas station attendant. Another example of the Prayer of Binding and Loosing -

"Heavenly Father, I bring before you my child who is not walking in your ways. Right now, in the name of Jesus I call to attention and summon you spirits of sexual lust, perversion, partying, rebellion disobedience, smoking and lying that have taken my child hostage. Jesus Christ died for the salvation of my child, and His blood was shed for the freedom of my child. I now in the authority of the blood of Jesus, and in the name of Jesus, arrest all your activities against my child and command you to cease in your operations and stop your manoeuvres. I now loose and release the power of the Holy Spirit, to convict them and turn my child's life around in the name of Jesus. I now loose the mighty angels of God, to go and exterminate and destroy all relationships that they are in, that connect them to evil in the name of Jesus. I now also release the angels to release godly men and women into their lives that have a key to their heart and destiny - men and women that they will listen to, men and women who are packaged for them. I now command this into manifestation in the name of Jesus."

When praying the Prayer of Binding and Loosing, it is advisable to spend some time in praise and worship so you can be surrounded by the presence of God, if the presence is not already on you. It is best to pray this prayer in the presence of God, as this will give your prayer more power. It is also best to follow this prayer with praying in the spirit with fervency and intensity. I encourage you to use this prayer now and turn the tide of battle in your favour.

Please note that in the Prayer of Binding and loosing you don't ask God to bind or loose for you. He will not do that as you have dominion on the earth. Asking the Lord to bind a devil for you in your life, church and in your nation, is like calling your landlord who is in America from Kingston, Jamaica and asking him to fly down, bring spray with him and come and kill a cockroach that is under your bed. Your landlord will not do that because you can handle it yourself, by using your authority to get the cockroach out. There are demonic cockroaches in the different rooms of your life, and instead of screaming and jumping on your bed and asking God to help you, use your authority, use the power He has given you and kill every demonic cockroach in your life, in the name of Jesus.

I prophesy that the anointing of God will come on you now, and you will rise up like a mighty warrior and use the insecticide of binding and loosing against every demonic cockroach found in every room in your life. I see a spiritual, nuclear Holy Ghost bomb go off against the forces of darkness in your life, in Jesus' name. Amen.

Prayer

Holy Spirit, teach me how to pray the Prayer of Binding and Loosing in all aspects of my life, so that I may walk in victory over the forces of darkness.

Today's Assignment

Stop and reflect on whether you waste time in prayer, talking to the Heavenly Father about demonic cockroaches that you should eliminate and bind in Jesus' name.

Day 21

The Prayer of Decree and Declarations releases God's Rhema to activate the supernatural on your behalf

Job 22:27-29 Thou shalt make thy prayer unto him, and he shall hear thee, and thou shalt pay thy vows. (28) Thou shalt also decree a thing, and it shall be established unto thee: and the light shall shine upon thy ways. (29) When men are cast down, then thou shalt say, There is lifting up; and he shall save the humble person.

The Prayer of Decree and Declaration is the sword of the spirit described in Ephesians 6:17 "And take the helmet of salvation and the sword of the spirit which is the word of God."

The Greek for 'word' in the scripture is the word *'rhema'* which means the spoken word of God. This is a specific word from the bible, or the voice of God concerning the outcome of a situation.

This word is given to you to declare in the realm of the spirit and the realm of the natural. When decreed, and declared with power and intention as often as required, it releases the creative power of God to come into manifestation.

The Rhema of God breathed into the human heart, conceived, formed and spoken with the human tongue without doubt and fear, releases the creative power of God.

This Prayer of Decree and Declaration was in effect when God spoke to Abram and told him to change his name to Abraham, which meant 'the father of many nations,' when he was still childless.

He also said that Sarai must be changed to Sarah, which means 'mother of many nations.' That was the wisdom of God, causing Sarai and Abram to make a declaration whenever they called each other by their new names.

Gen 17:1-6 "And when Abram was ninety years old and nine, the LORD appeared to Abram, and said unto him, I am the Almighty God; walk before me, and be thou perfect. (2) And I will make my covenant between me and thee, and will multiply thee exceedingly. (3) And Abram fell on his face: and God talked with him, saying, (4) As for me, behold, my covenant is with thee, and thou shalt be a father of many nations. (5) Neither shall thy name any more be called Abram, but thy name shall be Abraham; for a father of many nations have I made thee. (6) And I will make thee exceeding fruitful, and I will make nations of thee, and kings shall come out of thee."

Gen 17:15-18 "And God said unto Abraham, As for Sarai thy wife, thou shalt not call her name Sarai, but Sarah shall her name be. (16) And I will bless her, and give thee a son also of her: yea, I will bless her, and she shall be a mother of nations; kings of people shall be of her. (17) Then Abraham fell upon his face, and laughed, and said in his heart, Shall a child be born unto him that is an hundred years old? and shall Sarah, that is ninety years old, bear? (18) And Abraham said unto God, O that Ishmael might live before thee!"

As you can see from the scripture, Abraham had a major problem in believing that he would conceive a child with Sarah. So, God by His wisdom corrected the problem by having them declare His promise every time they spoke to each other. Every time one of Abraham's servants or friends called them, they would declare the word of God over their lives; that they would be the father and mother of many nations. Somewhere during the declaring of God's promise with their mouths, the creative power of God to make it happen was released.

Many of us think directly opposite to the way the Kingdom of God operates. When God shows us something in our hearts that He wants to do for us, we hesitate to say it in case it doesn't happen. We don't know that we need to declare it for it to happen.

Elohim, the God of the heaven and the earth, needed the faith and the words of Abraham and Sarah to do His great work amongst them.

He may have shown you His plans for your life and you are waiting on Him to make it happen. The opposite is true; He is waiting on you to declare it in the presence of opposing circumstances, so his creative power may be released.

You may ask, "How often should I pray the Prayer of Declaration?" That's very easy. You stop declaring when you see what you are declaring, manifest in the natural. This is a prayer to be repeated again and again and again.

So, it's time to write down all the promises God has made to you, all the things God has shown you in the spirit, and start declaring them over your life every day.

In the book of Job, it states that 'thou shall decree a thing and it shall be established.' This thing that you decree is not chosen by you, but it is revealed to you by the Rhema word - and it becomes unto you the sword of the spirit with which you attack and take new territory.

The Prayer of Declaration and Decree is offensive. It has the power to slice demons and it works in harmony with the Prayer of Thanksgiving, Praise and Worship.

As you engage in the Prayer of Thanksgiving, Praise and Worship until God's tangible presence shows up, and then you declare the Rhema word, creative power is released. So, start decreeing and declaring what God is saying to you about your future.

I love the part of the scripture in Job 22 which states that 'when men say there is a casting down, God shall say there is a lifting up.'

It literally means that when people are speaking the language of their circumstances and environment, the informed sense of God will decree the Rhema word, which will be the opposite. When men declare that you are finished, you declare by the Rhema word that you are just beginning.

When the doctor declares that you have a terminal disease, you declare that by the stripes of Jesus, you are healed. When men say that there is famine and recession in the land, you declare that you will make your first million this year.

Prayer

Heavenly Father, please bring to my remembrance, through the Holy Spirit, every Rhema word and promise You have made to me that I have forgotten. I need to start declaring Your word, because declaration is my responsibility, whilst performing Your word that I have declared in faith is Your responsibility.

Today's Assignment

Write in a journal all the promises that God has made to you that you need to start declaring.

Day 22

The Prayer of Supplication is a written legal case for divine intervention that you present before the throne of God in serious circumstances

Phil 4:6-7 Be careful for nothing; but in every thing by prayer and supplication with thanksgiving let your requests be made known unto God. (7) And the peace of God, which passeth all understanding, shall keep your hearts and minds through Christ Jesus.

There are times when you are faced with serious situations in your lives that require you to go before the throne of grace with a legal request, based on the knowledge of the scriptures.

The Prayer of Supplication is required when you need the intervention of divine justice and you want Elohim, the judge of the heavens and the earth, to decree judgement in your favour.

73

With this prayer, you find some scriptures that apply to your case, and you carefully write out the prayer with the supporting scriptures, making sure it is as strong as possible. Then after a praise and worship session, you would take it before God, read out your written petition and submit it to God for His intervention.

This is not a prayer that you pray every day. It's a prayer that you use when the long arm of divine justice is required to bring things to divine order.

The last time I prayed this type of prayer was about three years ago, when a small group of jealous and envious preachers had sought to scandal and propagate lies and rumours about me, in a bid to undermine my rising influence.

I did not react in the flesh, but went into the book of Psalms and found the most lethal scriptures that David prayed concerning his enemies, and packaged them together in a written petition before God. I knew that my heart was right with God, and I knew that what they were saying were lies and twisted facts, so I could pray with boldness. I set aside a time to pray, praised and worshipped, and then I laid out my petition and it was over. I never touched the subject again. All I can tell you is that they evaporated from my environment.

I also remember another incident when I made a petition before God. This is when one of my daughters had just gone into secondary school, and I saw that an evil spirit had entered into her. I remembered the Lord asking me to build a university for Him that would train believers to be labourers in the end time harvest. I said yes to His request, but then asked Him if He could do something for me as well, which was to deliver my daughter from the generational curse of rebellion.

I told the Lord that He did not have to say yes to my request; that I would still do what He asked me to do. He said yes, and my daughter was gloriously delivered and went on to lead over a thousand people to Jesus Christ.

As you can see it's a prayer that is best used to provoke divine intervention that brings judgement to the enemies of God's plan for your life.

Prayer

Holy Spirit, I ask that you lead and guide me when I should use the Prayer of Supplication to bring divine justice into my circumstances.

Today's Assignment

Stop and reflect on a scenario in your past that the Prayer of Supplication would have made a difference.

Day 23

The Prayer of Agreement increases the spiritual power available for manifestation among a few people

Matt 18:19-20 Again I say unto you, That if two of you shall agree on earth as touching anything that they shall ask, it shall be done for them of my Father which is in heaven. (20) For where two or three are gathered together in my name, there am I in the midst of them.

There are times when the faith required to receive an answer from God in a timely manner is not fully in your possession. This is when you can join with someone else and add their faith to your faith - so that your collective faith will be able to release the prayer with the required fervency and power to receive the answer that is required.

The Prayer of Agreement is unique in that all the other types of prayer, apart from the Unified Prayer, can be prayed with the Prayer of Agreement. That is, someone who is synchronized in the spirit with you can be added to the prayer session.

Let me explain the conditions of a successful Prayer of Agreement.

1. There must be unity in the spirit between the parties involved. There can be no unforgiveness, bitterness or unresolved issues with the parties involved.
2. The parties involved must have passion for the primary prayer to get the prayer answered.
3. The persons must possess faith to add to your faith.

The scripture says that when two or three are gathered in the name of Jesus, God is in the midst. When God is in the midst of people in agreement, and the above conditions are met, He is there to release divine acceleration and intervention. This prayer is an obvious prayer that engaged and married couples, families, destiny friends and partners in a ministry should be able to pray with good effect.

However, the devil knows this and is always sowing division among the spiritually illiterate, to stop them from meeting the conditions and having a successful Prayer of Agreement.

My counsel to you is that you need to protect the agreement in the spirit with your divine relationships.

Prayer

Holy Spirit, I ask that You teach me to use the Prayer of Agreement, which is a turbo boost to get my prayers answered quicker and faster.

Today's Assignment

Stop and reflect on any issues in your life in which the Prayer of Agreement will help bring divine intervention faster.

Day 24

Prayer of Consecration and Dedication is voluntarily submitting to the will of God in a situation

Luke 22:41-44 And he was withdrawn from them about a stone's cast, and kneeled down, and prayed, (42) Saying, Father, if thou be willing, remove this cup from me: nevertheless not my will, but thine, be done. (43) And there appeared an angel unto him from heaven, strengthening him. (44) And being in an agony he prayed more earnestly: and his sweat was as it were great drops of blood falling down to the ground.

During the course of walking in our divine destiny, there are seasons that we all face when the will of God and God's plan are repulsive to our flesh.

These are times when disciplining our flesh and making it obey God's will can be so difficult. Every person born of a woman who seeks to do God's will faces moments like that in their journey of destiny.

Jesus faced this moment in the Garden of Gethsemane when His emotions, His mind and His body reacted against going through the process of being crucified on the cross. His spirit was willing but His flesh was begging for an exit. This is when Jesus prayed the Prayer of Consecration and Dedication. In this prayer, you make your body a living sacrifice unto the Lord. You give your body as a living bond offering unto the Lord.

This is what Jesus said, even though He came with the mission to die on the cross. He said "Father, if it be possible, let this cup pass away from me." This language and metaphor is very unfamiliar to people who grew up in the west. The bible is not a western book; it's a book from the south, and I grew up in the southern part of Africa, where everyone would have understood what Jesus was saying.

In the south, parents, particularly those who still value their roots in the health traditions of their forefathers, would mix the most detestable smelling and tasting concoction of herbs for children to drink to make them strong. I had to suffer that at the hands of my grandfather, with a huge iron mug that I thought you could fit a small head in. Many of the medications and vitamins used today came from the roots and herbs that grew in the south. Our forefathers had knowledge of this and would take some of their roots and herbs, and boil them without sugar to be drunk raw for the benefit of their health. All the children, even the obedient ones, would look to their parents or grandparents to see if they really had to drink the concoctions, and their answer was always in the affirmative.

Jesus found himself in this same situation. The cup was a bitter cup to drink from to redeem and rescue mankind from the curse of sin and the power of Satan. I am glad that He drank the drink in the cup called the Cross and the Crucifixion. "Nevertheless, not my will but thy will be done."

Jesus, in speaking to the disciples, said in Matthew 17:24-27 "And when they were come to Capernaum, they that received tribute *money* came to Peter, and said, Doth not your master pay tribute? (25) He saith, Yes. And when he was come into the house, Jesus prevented him, saying, What thinkest thou, Simon? of whom do the kings of the earth take custom or tribute? of their own children, or of strangers? (26) Peter saith unto him, Of strangers. Jesus saith unto him, Then are the children free. (27) Notwithstanding, lest we should offend them, go thou to the sea, and cast an hook, and take up the fish that first cometh up; and when thou hast opened his mouth, thou shalt find a piece of money: that take, and give unto them for me and thee."

Jesus made it clear that anyone who followed Him would have moments in his or her life, when he or she must take up his or her cross. It simply means, crucifying your selfish desires, thoughts and emotions for God's greater will to be done in your life.

So far in my life, I have only had to go to that place three times. The first occurred when I obeyed the call of God and His instruction to stop pursuing a Bachelor of Science Degree in Civil Engineering and become a Minister. This action displeased my father because it went against his command, and I was subsequently thrown out of the house and lost my weekly allowance and inheritance, which was quite significant at that time.

I was raised up in a house of privilege with chauffeurs, security guards, maids and house servants. But now I had no money, I had to go and live with my granddad, and my mum had to hide and bring me things. This was a tough place to be in and a tough time in my life. I had previously received a one week encounter with the Lord, where night after night I was taken into the visions of the Lord, and my destiny of becoming a Prophet was revealed to me. I knew that God did not want me to become a Civil Engineer, and sitting in that classroom was not God's plan for my life.

At that time, no one in my family was saved, so my decision resulted in an international family conference that was held between Free Town, Sierra Leone and Bagul, Gambia. This was held to discuss what type of madness had come over the eldest child of the leading family in the Thomas clan. It was a hellish time, because not only was I going against the educational track my family had envisioned for me, but I was breaking the legacy of Free Masonry in my family.

My paternal grandfather was the leader of the masonic lodge in Sierra Leonne, and had handed the baton to my father after his death. I was the heir apparent and a Pentecostal tongue talking Holy Ghost fire preacher, and this was not compatible with the legacy of Free Masonry. This was a tsunami in the family.

However, the Lord told me that if I obey Him, my suffering will be a seed that will reap the harvest of salvation in my family. This has come to pass and from Free Town to Bagul, the wind of the spirit blew, and the sons and daughters of the Thomas clan received Jesus as their Lord and Saviour, and are working the works of God. My sister and her husband lead a great ministry, and are the owners of a Christian television station that reaches the nation.

The other two moments occurred in the last five years of my life. I am so glad that when those times came and my flesh said no, I knelt before God and re-consecrated my life to Him.

In summary, the Prayer of Consecration and Dedication is prayed when your flesh is rebelling against the will of God for your life, and in the prayer, you decide by your word, to choose God's will, God's plan and God's way. He then responds and gives you the grace to walk through the temporal suffering.

Prayer

Holy Spirit, guide me, teach me and empower me to pray the Prayer of Consecration and Dedication when my flesh rebels against Your will.

Today's Assignment

Stop and reflect on a moment of your life when the Prayer of Consecration and Dedication would have empowered you to do God's will.

Day 25

The Prayer of Thanksgiving, Praise and Worship brings a Manifestation of God into your situation

Psa 22:2-3 O my God, I cry in the daytime, but thou hearest not; and in the night season, and am not silent. (3) But thou art holy, O thou that inhabitest the praises of Israel.

The Prayer of Thanksgiving, Praise and Worship from a sincere heart will always bring God's presence into manifestation. However, thanksgiving, praise and worship are not the same thing.

Thanksgiving

Thanksgiving is the joyful, sincere, grateful giving of thanks to God for what He has done, and what He is doing in your life.

Psa 100:1-5 states "Make a joyful noise unto the LORD, all ye lands. (2) Serve the LORD with gladness: come before his presence with singing. (3) Know ye that the LORD he *is* God: *it is* he *that* hath made us, and not we ourselves; *we are* his people, and the sheep of his pasture. (4) Enter into his gates with thanksgiving, *and* into his courts with praise: be thankful unto him, *and* bless his name. (5) For the LORD *is* good; his mercy *is* everlasting; and his truth *endureth* to all generations."

The above scripture reveals to us the protocol for approaching our God, who is the King of Kings and Lord of Lords. It starts by entering His presence with singing. Therefore, joyful singing is a corridor for the presence of God where prayer is answered.

It then instructs us to enter the gates of God's temple and habitation through thanksgiving. Thanksgiving is the password that must be keyed in, to enter through the gates of God's habitation.

Praise

Praise is different from thanksgiving. It is the exaltation of God for who He is. It is proclaiming and declaring His greatness above every situation and scenario on earth, in heaven and under the earth. We thank God for what He has done and we praise God for who He is.

The scripture states that let everything that has breath praise the Lord. When thanksgiving moves into praise,

God comes into the midst of it and that's when worship can begin.

Worship

Worship is man's reverent, ecstatic response to the greatness, love and glory of God. Worship is a response to God's presence; you cannot truly worship except He comes. You can thank Him and praise Him until He manifests - but when He does, worship begins, because worship is love responding to love. It is man's reverence to God's greatness; there is no ritual for worship.

People cry, kneel and roll on the floor in worship, people whisper in worship and tremble under the power of God.

This prayer of thanksgiving, praise and worship releases the presence of God into your life, which sends demons packing, flattens mountains, destroys barriers and makes you more like the One you worshipped. Oh how great thou art My Lord!

Prayer

Holy Spirit, grace me with a lifestyle of thanksgiving, praise and worship, as that is the lifestyle of living in Your presence. In Jesus' name. Amen.

Today's Assignment

Stop and reflect on how often you praise and worship God when you are home alone. You should do it daily.

Day 26

Corporate and Unified prayer release a higher release of the Kingdom of the Supernatural in the earth

Acts 4:23-35 And being let go, they went to their own company, and reported all that the chief priests and elders had said unto them. (24) And when they heard that, they lifted up their voice to God with one accord, and said, Lord, thou art God, which hast made heaven, and earth, and the sea, and all that in them is: (25) Who by the mouth of thy servant David hast said, Why did the heathen rage, and the people imagine vain things? (26) The kings of the earth stood up, and the rulers were gathered together against the Lord, and against his Christ. (27) For of a truth against thy holy child Jesus, whom thou hast anointed, both Herod, and Pontius Pilate, with the Gentiles, and the people of Israel, were gathered together, (28) For to do whatsoever thy hand and thy counsel determined before to be done. (29) And now, Lord, behold their threatenings: and grant unto thy servants, that with all boldness they may speak thy word, (30) By stretching forth thine hand to heal; and that signs and wonders may be done by the name of thy holy child Jesus. (31) And when they had prayed, the place was shaken where they were assembled together; and they were all filled with the Holy Ghost, and they spake the word of God with boldness. (32) And the multitude of them that believed were of one heart and of one soul: neither said any of them that ought of the things which he possessed was his own; but they had all things common. (33) And with great power gave the apostles witness of the resurrection of the Lord Jesus: and great grace was upon them all. (34) Neither was there any among them that lacked: for as many as were possessors of lands or houses sold them, and brought the prices of the things that were sold, (35) And laid them down at the apostles' feet: and distribution was made unto every man according as he had need.

The prayer that releases the greatest measure of anointing, the greatest measure of power, the greatest measure of divine intervention and the greatest measure of glory is the Unified Corporate Prayer.

What is released in those moments is greater than the individual anointing or the Prayer of Agreement. It is called the Corporate Anointing. In that moment, all the anointing, faith and power of the congregation merge into one, and heaven kisses earth with breakthroughs, revelations, interventions and glory. The church needs to pray corporately more often.

91

However, the unified prayer meeting in churches is not in fashion in most places today. The seeker- sensitive churches that do not want to do anything that may appear strange to the spiritually uneducated, have relegated unified praying in other tongues, in declarations and intercessions to a few old ladies that meet once a month in the church basement.

Such strong prayers are not fashionable for some of our modern-day people pleasing pastors.

However, the church in the book of Acts made United Prayer a part of their lifestyle and it brought them great victory. In the above scripture, United Prayer caused a release of -

1. A major healing anointing.
2. A prosperity anointing that was so great that there was no lack in the church.
3. An explosion of the spirit of giving.
4. Greater power and anointing among the disciples.
5. The multiplication of the church with new believers.

Oh, how we need these same occurrences today. However, there is only one way to achieve this, and that is through United Prayer. In most churches, the prayer meeting is the least attended meeting of all the services, when it is the meeting that generates the power whereby the other meetings draw from.

Let us get back to the Unified Corporate Prayer.

Prayer

Oh, Holy Spirit lead me to a congregation that honours and celebrates Unified Prayer, so that I can benefit from its power. In Jesus' name. Amen.

Today's Assignment

Stop and reflect on when last you participated in a real hot Unified Prayer meeting that left you intoxicated. Note this, when you join your fire with other saints, it makes your fire shine brighter. You will always leave a hot, spirit led prayer meeting better than you came.

Day 27

The need for Corporate United Prayer is very crucial for the saints to experience victory in the end of the last days

Acts 4:23-35 And being let go, they went to their own company, and reported all that the chief priests and elders had said unto them. (24) And when they heard that, they lifted up their voice to God with one accord, and said, Lord, thou art God, which hast made heaven, and earth, and the sea, and all that in them is: (25) Who by the mouth of thy servant David hast said, Why did the heathen rage, and the people imagine vain things? (26) The kings of the earth stood up, and the rulers were gathered together against the Lord, and against his Christ. (27) For of a truth against thy holy child Jesus, whom thou hast anointed, both Herod, and Pontius Pilate, with the Gentiles, and the people of Israel, were gathered together, (28) For to do whatsoever thy hand and thy counsel determined before to be done. (29) And now, Lord, behold their threatenings: and grant unto thy servants, that with all boldness they may speak thy word, (30) By stretching forth thine hand to heal; and that signs and wonders

may be done by the name of thy holy child
Jesus. (31) And when they had prayed, the place was
shaken where they were assembled together; and they
were all filled with the Holy Ghost, and they spake the
word of God with boldness. (32) And the multitude of
them that believed were of one heart and of one soul:
neither said any of them that ought of the things which
he possessed was his own; but they had all things
common. (33) And with great power gave the apostles
witness of the resurrection of the Lord Jesus: and great
grace was upon them all. (34) Neither was there any
among them that lacked: for as many as were
possessors of lands or houses sold them, and brought
the prices of the things that were sold, (35) And laid
them down at the apostles' feet: and distribution was
made unto every man according as he had need.

The end of the last days will be days of great battle,
persecution, famine and the distress of nations. It will
also be marked by the level of gross darkness and
ignorance about the realm of the spirit and the
supernatural. The ignorance of spiritual things will
make men and women as vulnerable as a lamb in front
of a hyena.

The church will need to step up its prayer meetings and
increase their frequency. There will be ministers who
will receive a calling to have 24-hour nonstop prayer.

I have participated in a ministry that had a calling to
pray 24 hours, 365 days of the year. It was great

attending meetings at one o' clock in the morning and staying until five o' clock praying with them. I believe we will see more of this type of operation in the spirit as the end draws nigh.

At any time of the day you can join the on-going praise and worship prayer meeting and short preaching session. May God multiply such 24-hour prayer assemblies globally.

Isa 62:6 states "I have set watchmen upon thy walls, O Jerusalem, *which* shall never hold their peace day nor night: ye that make mention of the LORD, keep not silence."

I believe that the Lord is raising up anointed people from the body of Christ with the mantle of a prayer watchman, and they will not cease to cry out night and day, until the Lord's plans for a glorious church and nations are established on the earth.

Everyone must pray to see God's plan be done in his or her life. However, there are some who have a special calling to be Prayer Watchmen.

These have been given gifts to perceive what God wants to do corporately for the church in a geographical location, and take the responsibility of praying it into manifestation. They also will see what the devil wants to do against the corporate church and will have the authority to bind it and loose the angels of God in response. If you are reading this book and you are called to be a Prayer Watchman, then I release a fresh anointing of God's grace on you. You are important to God's agenda being done on the earth.

While there are others who focus on praying for their own affairs and responsibilities, you have been given a special anointing to not only pray for your affairs and responsibilities, but for the things God wants to do corporately on the earth.

Treasure the calling. Most of the work is done in the hidden place where the eyes of man cannot see. But know this, on that day when you stand before the judgement seat of Christ, if you have been faithful to pray the corporate agenda God gave you, your reward will be great. This is because your faithfulness to prayer opened the door for God to intervene in the nations of the world to save, deliver and redeem.

Prayer

Heavenly Father, I ask that You put on me your Spirit of prayer, that I may cry out to You night and day in the name of Jesus.

Today's Assignment

What action are you going to take to participate in united prayer meetings more often?

Day 28

The Prayer of Enquiry is standing before God to receive divine direction, revelation and supernatural breakthrough formulas.

2 Sam 5:17-20; "When the Philistines heard that David had been anointed king over Israel, they went up in full force to search for him, but David heard about it and went down to the stronghold. Now the Philistines had come and spread out in the Valley of Rephaim; so David inquired of the Lord, "Shall I go and attack the Philistines? Will you deliver them into my hands?" The Lord answered him, "Go, for I will surely deliver the Philistines into your hands." So David went to Baal Perazim, and there he defeated them. He said, "As waters break out, the Lord has broken out against my enemies before me." So that place was called Baal Perazim. The Philistines abandoned their idols there, and David and his men carried them off. Once more the Philistines came up and spread out in the Valley of

Rephaim; so David inquired of the Lord, and he answered, "Do not go straight up, but circle around behind them and attack them in front of the poplar trees. As soon as you hear the sound of marching in the tops of the poplar trees, move quickly, because that will mean the Lord has gone out in front of you to strike the Philistine army." So David did as the Lord commanded him, and he struck down the Philistines all the way from Gibeon to Gezer."

There are moments in life when what you require is not for God to do something for you, but instead you require God to show you something. You need revelation -

- As to the mystery behind a stubborn problem.
- On the type of career to pursue.
- On the purpose and gifts that God has given you.
- On what church to attend and what city to live in.
- On your covenant friendships.
- On where God has preserved the anointing.
- On the location of your destiny money.
- On the identity, location and arrival of your spouse.
- On when to get married, how many children to have, and when to have them.

There is a myriad of scenarios that would occur in your life when you will need God to reveal something, expose something, interpret something, decode something or unearth something.

The prayer you pray to activate this is called the Prayer of Enquiry. In this prayer, you ask God for the information you need, and keep praying in the spirit continually until it is revealed to you.

Jesus in referring to this type of praying said "Ask and you shall receive, seek and ye shall find, knock and it shall be opened unto you."

The prayer of seeking and finding is called the Prayer of Enquiry.

Prayer

Holy Spirit, teach me how to use the Prayer of Enquiry when it is necessary for my breakthrough. In Jesus' name.

Today's Assignment

Stop and reflect on a scenario in your life that requires the Prayer of Enquiry.

Day 29

Fasting and Prayer releases breakthrough supernatural power to defeat stubborn problems

Matt 17:14-21 And when they were come to the multitude, there came to him a certain man, kneeling down to him, and saying, (15) Lord, have mercy on my son: for he is lunatick, and sore vexed: for ofttimes he falleth into the fire, and oft into the water. (16) And I brought him to thy disciples, and they could not cure him. (17) Then Jesus answered and said, O faithless and perverse generation, how long shall I be with you? how long shall I suffer you? bring him hither to me. (18) And Jesus rebuked the devil; and he departed out of him: and the child was cured from that very hour. (19) Then came the disciples to Jesus apart, and said, Why could not we cast him out? (20) And Jesus said unto them, Because of your unbelief: for verily I say unto you, If ye have faith as a grain of mustard seed, ye shall say unto this mountain, Remove hence to yonder place; and it shall remove; and nothing shall be impossible unto you. (21) Howbeit this kind goeth not out but by prayer and fasting.

The above scripture teaches us the priceless lesson on the laws of divine intervention and the release of power. Nine of Jesus' apostles, who had previously been appointed and anointed to heal the sick and cast out devils, could not cast out a demon out of a young boy. They sweated, prayed, declared, decreed, repented, praised, worshipped, enquired, and yet nothing happened. And to their utter surprise, Jesus came down and cast the devil out without strenuous efforts. They were perplexed and asked the Lord why they were not able to cast out this particular demon. Jesus' answer stands out and merits close examination. Jesus' reply was that this kind of demon or this kind of problem, bondage, situation, challenge, obstacle, or this kind of barrier, goeth not, dissolveth not and eliminateth not, but by prayer and fasting.

In this statement, he revealed that fasting can turbo boost and supercharge your prayers to deal with stubborn problems and demons.

"What is fasting?" you may ask. It is the abstinence of food for the focus of prayer, and for the intervention of God and the manifestation of His glory.

In writing this book I could not help but think of one of my female mentees in the ministry, who was born-again, loved God and was anointed for exploits, but yet had a nymphomaniac demon attached to her. She shared with me that she could not control her sexual urges and was extremely promiscuous, and no amount of praying or repenting could break it even after she was saved.

When that demon was in manifestation, it didn't take much for her to have sexual intercourse with the person of her interest.

This was a sad problem that caused her great pain. After doing everything, reading the scriptures and having no relief, she was led by the Spirit to do a forty-day fast to break the power of it. After the fast ended, it subsided but did not go away. She had to go on another forty-day fast. That is when it left her life forever. It has been over twenty years since that situation happened and she has been free and pure.

Some would shake their heads and wonder, "My Lord, is that what it takes to break stubborn problems?" The answer is yes.

Your problem might not be sex addiction, but it might be chronic poverty, stagnation, fear, constant changing emotions, romantic disasters, continual physical sicknesses, demonic attacks, demonic dream penetration, witchcraft, lying and all types of evil that manifest as a stubborn problem and stronghold in your life.

Prayer

Holy Spirit, show me when I need to add fasting to my prayers to deal with stubborn problems that my prayers alone cannot handle. In Jesus' name. Amen.

Today's Assignment

Stop and reflect on if there are any stubborn issues in your life that may require fasting and prayer.

Day 30

Fasting and praying strengthens our spirit man to receive higher level revelation.

Isa 58:6-14 Is not this the fast that I have chosen? to loose the bands of wickedness, to undo the heavy burdens, and to let the oppressed go free, and that ye break every yoke? (7) Is it not to deal thy bread to the hungry, and that thou bring the poor that are cast out to thy house? when thou seest the naked, that thou cover him; and that thou hide not thyself from thine own flesh? (8) Then shall thy light break forth as the morning, and thine health shall spring forth speedily: and thy righteousness shall go before thee; the glory of the LORD shall be thy reward. (9) Then shalt thou call, and the LORD shall answer; thou shalt cry, and he shall say, Here I am. If thou take away from the midst of thee the yoke, the putting forth of the finger, and speaking vanity; (10) And if thou draw out thy soul to the hungry, and satisfy the afflicted soul; then shall thy light rise in obscurity, and thy darkness be as the noonday: (11) And the LORD shall guide thee continually, and satisfy thy soul in drought, and make fat thy bones: and thou shalt be like a watered garden, and like a spring of water, whose waters fail

*not. (12) And they that shall be of thee shall build
the old waste places: thou shalt raise up the
foundations of many generations; and thou shalt be
called, The repairer of the breach, The restorer of paths
to dwell in. (13) If thou turn away thy foot from the
sabbath, from doing thy pleasure on my holy day; and
call the sabbath a delight, the holy of the LORD,
honourable; and shalt honour him, not doing thine
own ways, nor finding thine own pleasure, nor
speaking thine own words: (14) Then shalt thou
delight thyself in the LORD; and I will cause thee to
ride upon the high places of the earth, and feed thee
with the heritage of Jacob thy father: for the mouth of
the LORD hath spoken it.*

There are different types of fasts. I will explain them.

1. The Jesus Model Extended Fast

This is an extended fast which involves drinking water
and may last up to forty days. You must be led by the
spirit of God to do this fast and be given God's grace for
it. The longest I have fasted is twenty - one days with
water. Fasting is not dieting. It is denying your body
of food, so it can focus on the things of the spirit to
generate spiritual power, revelation and breakthrough.
Some people have been anointed to do this type of fast
without water. I have never done it. In the process of
writing this book, I'm about to do an extended fast, but
with water.

2. The Esther Fast

This fast is found in the book of Esther and its duration is three days. This is a total fast from food and work to seek the face of God for divine intervention or revelation.

3. The Daniel Fast

This is a fast found in the book of Daniel where he fasted for twenty-one days from meat, rice and carbohydrates. He just ate raw fruit and vegetables as he needed it, and spent the time praying and seeking God for supernatural illumination and breakthrough.

4. The Fasted Life

This is a lifestyle of fasting that is led by the Holy Spirit. It occurs regularly during every week of the year. You may fast for a few meals a day or two days a week, to seek the face of God for intimacy, empowerment and breakthrough. This is your lifestyle and you may wake up in the morning and decide to fast for breakfast and continue praying, then fast for lunch and continue praying. It's more of a lifestyle.

The first three types of fasting can be utilised according to the number of days you are led by the Spirit. You can choose to break your fast after a period of twelve hours e.g. six to six and start again the next day, or go through the days without breaking your fast.

The Lord will lead you according to your capacity, the urgency of the situation and the grace that is available to you. To live a supernatural life, fasting is not optional - it is a necessity.

It has the power to:

1. break strongholds in your life.
2. bring fresh revelation.
3. activate divine power.
4. cleanse you from spiritual toxins.
5. increase the presence of God in your life.
6. dismantle satanic barriers.
7. release the star in you.

One of the great benefits of fasting is that it teaches you discipline and impulse control. One of the greatest impulses is the God-given impulse to eat. Fasting subdues it and tells it that there will be no eating until you say so. The subduing of this God-given impulse empowers you after you fast to subdue any other evil impulses that may rise up in you.

Those who fast properly on a regular basis will develop greater self - control.

Prayer

Holy Spirit, empower me to subdue and overcome the desires of my flesh. In Jesus' name. Amen.

Today's Assignment

Stop and reflect on if there are any areas of your life where fasting can help you to develop.

Day 31

Wise people pray so they will know how to pray and not miss the target

Jas 4:1-3 From whence come wars and fightings among you? come they not hence, even of your lusts that war in your members? (2) Ye lust, and have not: ye kill, and desire to have, and cannot obtain: ye fight and war, yet ye have not, because ye ask not. (3) Ye ask, and receive not, because ye ask amiss, that ye may consume it upon your lusts.

We are now at the end of the book and you have learned about why prayer is important, watching in the spirit, the difference between the Logos word and the Rhema word, the twelve different types of prayer, and fasting and praying.

You may wonder why I did not mention Intercession. Because Intercessory Prayer is simply using any one of the prayers except for the Prayer of Salvation, the prayer of Repentance or the Prayer of Consecration, to pray for someone else. It is quite clear that you cannot pray the Prayer of Salvation for someone else, you cannot confess the sins of someone else, nor can you dedicate the will of someone else to do God's will.

When the other nine types of prayer are used to pray for other individuals, families, churches, nations or the world, it is called Intercession. When it is prayed for yourself, it is called petition.

Knowing what prayer to pray in a given scenario is a core secret to an effective prayer life. Therefore, wise people make a prayer of enquiry on what prayer to use, to pray about different situations they face, whether in petition or intercession.

Prayer

Oh, Holy Spirit, I make You my prayer partner today. Guide me into what prayers to use when I'm making personal petitions and intercessions. In the name of Jesus. Amen.

Today's Assignment

Stop and reflect on whether you ask the Holy Spirit to guide you before you begin to pray.

OTHER BOOKS BY ANDRE THOMAS

1. The Organizational Visionary
2. The Gift of Political Leadership
3. 12 Spheres of Leadership (The 12 types of leaders that shape the destinies of nations)
4. Unlock Your Greatness (A Young Leaders' Handbook)
5. Discovering Me
6. Uncommon Men and Distinguished Women
7. Coaching People into the 12 Spheres of Leadership
8. Seven Principles of Commonwealth Leadership
9. Discovering your Leadership Assignment
10. Preparing for your Leadership Assignment
11. Executing your Leadership Assignment
12. I Am a Leader (Inspiring Greatness in Kids)
13. The Entrepreneurial Visionary
14. The Social Visionary
15. From Brokenness to Wholeness
16. Wisdom for Leadership Coaches
17. Lessons from History for Policy Makers
18. Leading Nations into Economic Dignity

COMMISSION, VISION, MISSION AND MANDATE

Commission

Just as I called Moses to take a people from the land of bondage to Canaan, so have I called you to take a people from bondage to greatness.

Church Mandate

Build a network of Prophetic Assemblies called Divine Visitation Assemblies that take people from bondage to greatness.

Vision

To see a network of Prophetic Assemblies called Divine Visitation Assemblies take people from bondage to greatness.

Mission

To take a movement of people from bondage to greatness by the miracle power of God and leadership wisdom.

http://www.divinevisitation.com/

https://www.facebook.com/dvaonline/

ABOUT THE 12 SPHERES OF LEADERSHIP MOVEMENT

PURPOSE

To raise up a global movement of the 12 types of leaders that shape the destinies of nations.

OUR MISSION

To influence and empower two million leaders globally to execute divine assignments in the 12 spheres of leadership.

OUR METHOD

<u>Conferences</u>

To form strategic partnerships with key national leaders to hold 12 Spheres of Leadership conferences, events and speaking engagements.

Media and Communication

1. We create media programmes and a media platform to distribute 12 Spheres of Leadership Content to the World.
2. We communicate monthly to our partners through 'Leadership Fuel' - a monthly audio teaching and news digest.

Books

We write, publish and distribute books that influence and empower leaders globally to execute divine assignments in the 12 Spheres of leadership.

How can your church, town, city or nation be transformed by the 12 Spheres of Leadership Movement?

There are 3 different events that Bishop Andre Thomas may be booked for:

1. Leadership Wisdom Explosion

An event where:

- The biblical wisdom of the 12 Spheres of Leadership is imparted to equip the saints and to shape the destiny of their nation.
- Visionaries are refreshed by the Holy Spirit.
- This event can also be customized to focus on specific spheres of leadership.

2. Anointing Revival

An event where:

- A fresh anointing is imparted to people individually and in mass to unlock their God given greatness.
- The delivering and healing power of God is also administered to set people free from all bondage.

3. VisionFest

This event features the best of Anointing Revival and Leadership Explosion Event in one conference that catapults the saints into higher dimensions of leadership, breakthrough, freedom, influence and impact.

www.12slm.org

www.vision-fest.org

Made in the USA
Columbia, SC
10 November 2020

24213004R00068